D1159684

SPACE MYSTERIES

WHAT IS A BLACK HOLE?

Gareth Stevens
Publishing

BY GREG ROZA

Please visit our website, www.garethstevens.com. For a free color catalog of all our high-quality books, call toll free 1-800-542-2595 or fax 1-877-542-2596.

Library of Congress Cataloging-in-Publication Data

Roza, Greg.
What is a black hole / by Greg Roza.
   p. cm. — (Space mysteries)
Includes index.
ISBN 978-1-4339-9229-2 (pbk)
ISBN 978-1-4339-9230-8 (6-pack)
ISBN 978-1-4339-9228-5 (library binding)
1. Black holes (Astronomy) — Juvenile literature. 2. Astronomy — Juvenile literature. I. Roza, Greg. II. Title
QB843.B55 R69 2014
523.8'875—dc23

First Edition

Published in 2014 by
Gareth Stevens Publishing
111 East 14th Street, Suite 349
New York, NY 10003

Copyright © 2014 Gareth Stevens Publishing

Designer: Katelyn E. Reynolds
Editor: Therese Shea

Photo credits: Cover, p. 1 NASA/CXC/M. Weiss; cover, pp. 1, 3–32 (background texture) David M. Schrader/Shutterstock.com; p. 3–32 (fun fact graphic) © iStockphoto.com/spxChrome; p. 5 Oko Laa/Shutterstock.com; p. 7 NASA/JPL-Caltech; p. 9 NASA/JPL-Caltech/R. Hunt (SSC); p. 11 NASA/ESA/JHU/R. Sankrit & W. Blair; p. 13 Alainr/Wikipedia.com; p. 15 NASA and The Hubble Heritage Team (AURA/STScI); p. 17 NASA, ESA, and G. Bacon (STScI); pp. 19, 29 NASA; p. 21 Mark Garlick/Science Photo Library/Getty Images; p. 23 NASA's Goddard Space Flight Center; p. 25 NASA/CXC/NGST; p. 27 NASA/ESA/STScI.

Printed in the United States of America

CPSIA compliance information: Batch #CS13GS: For further information contact Gareth Stevens, New York, New York at 1-800-542-2595.

CONTENTS

Words in the glossary appear in **bold** type the first time they are used in the text.

UNDERSTANDING GRAVITY

Did you know **gravity** is what holds the universe together? The more mass an object has, the greater its gravitational force. Earth is so massive that its gravity is strong enough to keep you, your house, and everything else firmly on the planet's surface. Gravity gives you weight.

You'd weigh more on Jupiter, because it's the most massive planet in the **solar system**. The sun is so massive that its gravitational force keeps all the planets circling, or orbiting, around it.

OUT OF THIS WORLD!

Every object in the universe with mass attracts every other object with mass.

Our Solar System

Neptune

Saturn

Mars

asteroid belt

sun

Uranus

Mercury

Earth

Venus

Jupiter

CLEANING UP THE UNIVERSE

Imagine something that's so massive nothing can escape its gravitational force. That object is called a black hole. That's right—black holes aren't just science fiction.

Black holes suck up any object that gets too close. They're the vacuum cleaners of the universe! The gravity created by a black hole is so strong that not even light, the fastest thing in the universe, can escape it. Where do black holes come from? The answer is in the stars!

OUT OF THIS WORLD!

Black holes are very small compared to the amount of matter in them. A black hole with the same amount of matter as Earth would fit in the palm of your hand!

6

Most black holes are thought to come from stars.

THE LIVES OF STARS

A star begins life as a clump of swirling gas and dust. As this clump grows larger and more massive, its gravity increases and pulls in more matter. The clump spins and grows **denser**. Finally, it forms a glowing ball of gas called a star.

The gas hydrogen undergoes **nuclear fusion** inside a star. This process gives off energy in the form of heat and light. Nuclear fusion also balances out the force of gravity, which continues to pull matter toward the star's center.

OUT OF THIS WORLD!

The largest stars may only live for about 10 million years. A star the size of our sun lasts for about 10 billion years.

As the star forms, it gives off two jets of dust and gas, which you can see in this image.

9

DYING STARS

After millions or billions of years, a star uses up its hydrogen fuel and can no longer continue nuclear fusion. Gravity pulls much of the star's matter into a tight, dense center, called its core.

The sun is a small star. When it dies, it will shrink and cool. Much more massive stars, however, end life in a huge, incredibly bright explosion called a supernova. After that, the star's core may turn into a neutron star. But some stars turn into black holes.

OUT OF THIS WORLD!

A neutron star is a very small, very dense, and very hot star.

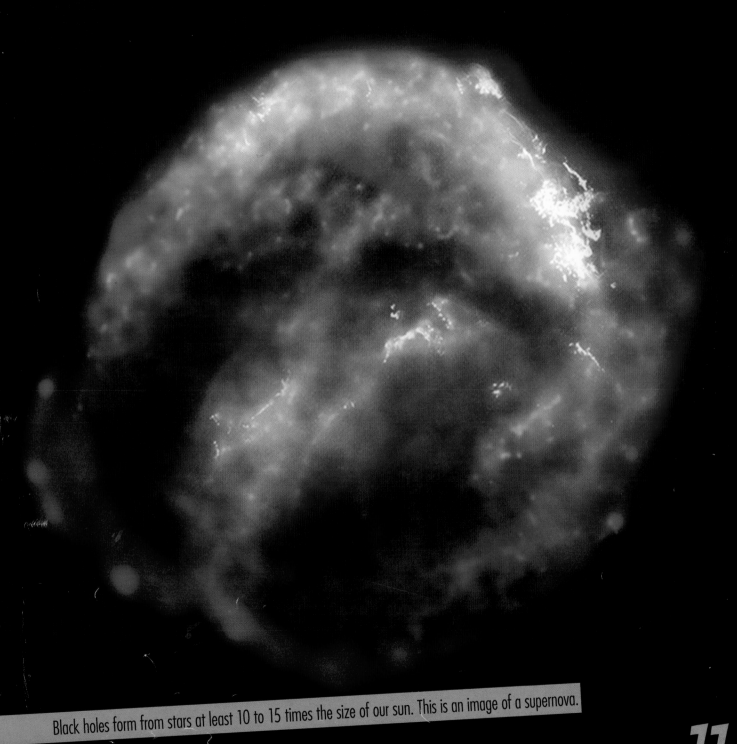

Black holes form from stars at least 10 to 15 times the size of our sun. This is an image of a supernova.

11

THE BIRTH OF BLACK HOLES

After a supernova, the core of some dying stars grows smaller. However, it continues to pull in matter as it shrinks, becoming denser and more massive. The gravity created by the shrinking core becomes enormous.

The gravity of the dying star becomes so great that not even light can escape it—and a black hole is born! This is why black holes look black to us. They would be invisible if we didn't have special tools to see them.

OUT OF THIS WORLD!

Black holes can be the size of a single atom or a million times larger than a star!

Black holes have no light, which is why they seem dark in images like this.

13

SUPERMASSIVE!

The largest black holes are called supermassive black holes. A very large black hole was discovered at the center of a **galaxy** about 336 **light-years** away. This monster black hole is 10 times larger than our solar system and has the mass of about 21 billion stars!

Many scientists think it's likely that supermassive black holes are at the center of every galaxy. They probably formed as the galaxy was forming. They may have grown so large by joining with other black holes.

OUT OF THIS WORLD!

The Schwarzschild **radius** is a measurement that shows how squeezed together, or compressed, an object needs to be to become a black hole.

14

Scientists think the bigger the galaxy is, the bigger the black hole found there.

ESCAPE VELOCITY

Escape velocity is the speed an object needs to be traveling to break free of the gravitational force of a planet, star, or moon. For example, a rocket needs to travel about 7 miles (11 km) a second to break free of Earth's gravity. That's 25,200 miles (40,555 km) per hour!

Light travels at about 186,000 miles (300,000 km) per second. When the escape velocity for a dying star is greater than the speed of light, a black hole forms.

OUT OF THIS WORLD!

Earth would need to be compressed to a radius of 0.35 inch (0.9 cm) to become a black hole!

Scientists discovered that a blue star has been tossed out of the center of the Milky Way with enough speed to break free of the galaxy's gravity!

17

EVENT HORIZON

It's possible to orbit a black hole without getting sucked into it. In fact, many black holes have a ring of matter orbiting them called an **accretion** disk.

The closer you get to a black hole, the greater its pull of gravity becomes. Finally, you'd reach an area called the outer event horizon. There, the black hole's force is strong, but it's still possible to get away. However, once you reach the inner event horizon, there's no turning back!

OUT OF THIS WORLD!

An event horizon is a kind of border. Beyond it, nothing can escape the force of gravity, not even light.

accretion disk

The accretion disk is one of the features of a black hole that help scientists locate it.

SINGULARITY

According to the laws of **physics**, once an object crosses the event horizon, it won't stop falling toward the center of the black hole. This is where the black hole's gravity is strongest.

The center of a black hole is called the singularity. It's a point where the density is **infinite** but the volume is zero. That means a limitless amount of matter fits in a space that doesn't exist. How can this be? That's a question scientists may never truly understand, either!

To understand what really happens inside a black hole, you'd have to be there. However, if you were inside a black hole, you'd never live to tell about it!

JETS OF ENERGY

While it's true that black holes suck up matter and grow denser, many also emit, or spit out, matter. Black holes emit high-speed jets of matter from their centers. Scientists think this might be caused by a **magnetic field** within the accretion disk.

Some black holes emit more matter than they gather. As this happens, they grow less massive, and their gravitational force decreases. This means that a black hole can disappear!

OUT OF THIS WORLD!

It would take billions and billions of years for a black hole to "evaporate"—probably more time than the universe has even existed!

THE PARTS OF A BLACK HOLE

accretion disk

singularity

jet of matter

event horizon

The jets created by black holes travel at close to the speed of light.

WHERE ARE THEY?

You might be wondering: If black holes are black, how do scientists find them? Scientists find and study black holes by observing and measuring the effects they have on the objects around them.

When a black hole sucks up matter, the matter heats up and gives off **X-rays** that scientists can measure. Scientists can also observe how a black hole's gravity affects other nearby objects. Stars near a black hole, for example, move much faster than those farther away.

OUT OF THIS WORLD!

Scientists have learned that the gravity of massive objects can bend light. This helps them find black holes.

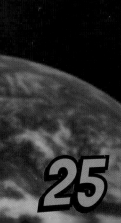

This is the Chandra X-ray Observatory. It finds X-ray sources within our solar system and billions of light-years away.

25

BLACK HOLES IN THE NEIGHBORHOOD

Most scientists believe there's a supermassive black hole at the heart of the Milky Way galaxy. They've observed about a dozen stars orbiting some unknown object there. The orbits are very fast. One star circles the black hole in about 11.5 years, traveling at about 3,100 miles (5,000 km) a second!

Scientists think the black hole at the center of the Milky Way has about 4 million times the mass of our sun. However, the closest black hole to Earth might be "just" 1,600 light-years away!

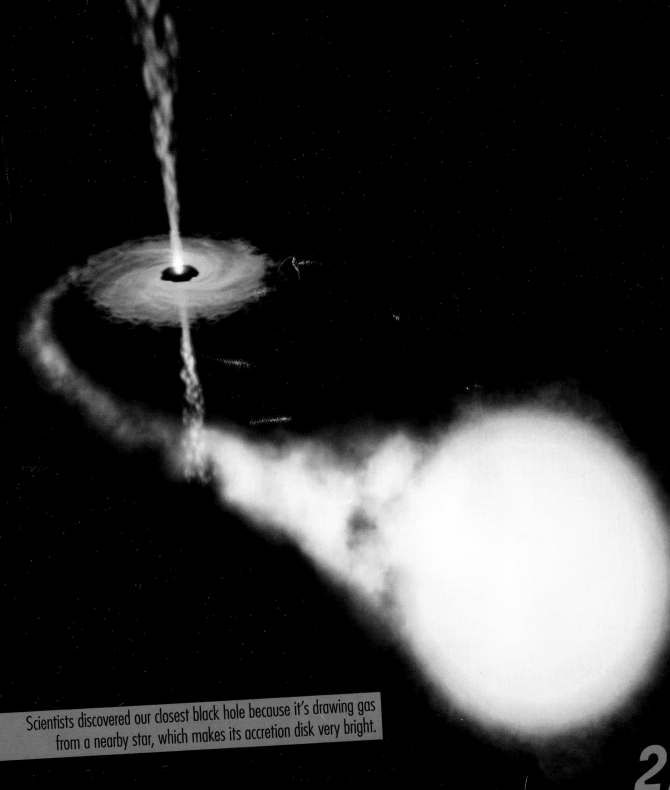

Scientists discovered our closest black hole because it's drawing gas from a nearby star, which makes its accretion disk very bright.

27

ARE BLACK HOLES DOORWAYS?

Though we're learning more about them all the time, black holes are one of the great mysteries of the universe. Many people, including scientists and science-fiction writers, have suggested that black holes are "wormholes," doorways to other locations in the universe—or perhaps to a universe other than our own.

As exciting as this idea sounds, many scientists think it's impossible. Since black holes are so hard to study, we may never know the real answer.

OUT OF THIS WORLD!

Some scientists suggest that every black hole has a white hole. That's a doorway where all the matter that gets sucked into a black hole escapes to.

In 2012, a black hole 17 billion times the mass of the sun was found. It's thought to be 4,000 times larger than the black hole at the center of the Milky Way!

29

GLOSSARY

accretion: a building up of matter

denser: having more matter in a given area

galaxy: a large group of stars, planets, gas, and dust that form a unit within the universe

gravity: the force that pulls objects toward the center of a planet or star

infinite: without limits, endless

light-year: the distance light can travel in 1 year

magnetic field: the area around a magnet or magnetic body where its pull is felt

nuclear fusion: a reaction during which the atoms of one element come together to make atoms of a heavier element

physics: the study of matter, energy, force, and motion, and the relationships among them

radius: the distance from the center of a circle or sphere to a point on the outer edge or surface

solar system: the sun and all the space objects that orbit it, including the planets and their moons

X-ray: a powerful type of energy that is similar to light but is invisible to the human eye

FOR MORE INFORMATION

BOOKS

Abramson, Andra Serlin. *Inside Stars*. New York, NY: Sterling Children's Books, 2011.

DeCristofano, Carolyn Cinami. *A Black Hole Is Not a Hole*. Watertown, MA: Charlesbridge, 2012.

Than, Ker. *Black Holes*. New York, NY: Children's Press, 2010.

WEBSITES

Black Holes
www.kidsastronomy.com/black_hole.htm
Learn more about black holes, and see some great images and videos that explain how they work.

Black Holes
science.nasa.gov/astrophysics/focus-areas/black-holes/
Read more about black holes at the NASA website.

INDEX